Me God's way

Dr. Chris Richards & Dr. Liz Jones

Published by:
EP Books (Evangelical Press), 1st Floor Venture House,
6 Silver Court,
Watchmead,
Welwyn Garden City
AL7 1TS

Published in association with:
Lovewise,
14 Portland Terrace,
Jesmond,
Newcastle upon Tyne
NE2 1QQ

This booklet contains chapter two of 'Growing up God's way' which is available for boys (ISBN 978-0-85234-999-1) and girls (ISBN 978-1-78397-000-1).

ISBN 978-1-78397-174-9

Why learn about marriage?

In His wisdom God has given us one basic design for forming a family; this design is based on marriage. Over the next few years you will make decisions that might affect whether it will be possible for you to have a family in the way God intends. You will need to think and act in a way that pleases God and not do anything that might spoil this opportunity.

For these reasons, it is important to learn about marriage now, even though actually getting married may seem a long way off.

Marriage - a special design

Have you ever seen a wedding? Did everyone seem very happy? Was there an exciting atmosphere? Yes, it is obvious to anyone at a wedding that it is a very special occasion. But this is not only because of the dress, confetti and cake; at a wedding the couple show their love for each other by starting the life-long relationship of marriage.

Marriage was designed by God. The first man and woman created by God, Adam and Eve, were also husband and wife, setting a pattern for men and women to follow in the future. These words from the first book of the Bible called Genesis show that this was God's intention:

For this reason a man will leave his father and mother and be united to his wife, and they will become one flesh.

Genesis 2:24 (NIV)

This is why marriage is known as a creation ordinance. A creation ordinance is an arrangement, designed by God, which has been present since the creation of the world. Marriage is recorded throughout history and in all the nations around the world, even by people who do not recognise God as its designer.

Marriage has been designed to be the basis of each family unit, so that children can be born into a family and benefit from the love and security of family life. This is the way that God has chosen to raise one generation after another to work and care for His world and so fulfil God's command to 'be fruitful and multiply and fill the earth and subdue it' (Genesis 1:28). Just as a building is made up of individual bricks, so God intends all nations and their communities to be made up of the building bricks of the family unit based on marriage. Without strong marriages, a country stops working properly and starts to fall apart.

Once we realise that God is the designer of marriage, is it any wonder that we get excited about a wedding when we see His design put into practice as a new family forms and a new unit of society takes shape?

Who can get married?

We can find the answer to this question by looking at God's own description of marriage in the verse which we have just read: 'a man will leave his father and mother and be united to his wife, and they will become one flesh' (Genesis 2:24 [NIV]).

From this, we learn that God designed marriage to be between a man and a woman. God has designed a man and a woman to be different – not only in their bodies, but also in how they feel and the way they think.

The differences between a man and woman allow them to take on different roles in marriage. God designed Eve to be Adam's helper and companion. It is God's intention that both the husband and the wife work together in a complementary way so that both they and their children benefit.

To complement means to act together in different ways for the good of both. As the head of the family, the husband should take the lead in providing for it, in protecting it from threats and in teaching his children. The wife should support her husband in these responsibilities, and take a greater part in running the home, and in feeding and caring for the family.

We also learn from this verse (Genesis 2:24) that God intends that there should be only one husband ('a man') and one wife ('his wife'). In addition, we observe that Adam and Eve were adults when they married. God intends marriage to be for those who have been through puberty, so that they are mature in the way they think and old enough to have children.

Leaving and uniting

The same verse shows other things about marriage as well. It states that, when a man marries, he is to 'leave his father and mother'. You might have noticed that, at a wedding, the bride walks in with her father and then walks out with her new husband. This represents an important part of getting married. The husband and wife must leave their parents and join together to form a new family as a married couple.

We also learn that when a man and a woman get married, they are 'united' in many important ways. They live together and share everything: food, money, surname, holidays... They share their thoughts in making decisions together. They also unite their bodies in special physical closeness, which the Bible describes as the two becoming 'one flesh'.

The order in which we do things is very important to God. In Genesis 2:24, the leaving of the family home is followed by uniting in marriage, which in turn is followed by the two becoming one flesh.

Today, many people in our society are choosing to go against this God-given order. Most commonly, they unite their bodies without getting married first. Others try to form a new family home before they have properly left their parents' home. Ignoring God's order in this way can lead to all kinds of problems.

The promises of marriage

Marriage is based on the promises that are made between a husband (bridegroom) and his wife (bride) on their wedding day. The bride and bridegroom usually give rings to each other and they wear these for the rest of their lives to remind them of the promises they have made. Because a ring does not have an end, it is a good example of the unending love between a husband and a wife.

These promises of marriage are very serious and are made before God and those present at the wedding; they are sometimes called 'vows'. A promise is the act of saying what you intend to do and then doing everything in your power to carry it out. When God makes a promise to His people, He always keeps it.

8

This is a mark of His faithfulness to us. Similarly, God requires us to keep our promises. In fact, a Christian should be known as one who keeps his or her promises, even when it hurts to do so (see Psalm 15:4). To say one thing but do another is one form of lying, which is forbidden by God in the ninth of the Ten Commandments, 'You shall not bear false witness against your neighbour' (Exodus 20:16). It is, therefore, important to think very seriously before making the promises of marriage.

Here is one version of the marriage vows spoken by the bride:

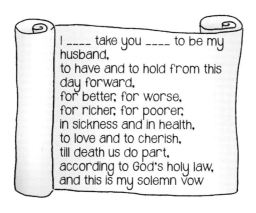

I ____ take you ____ to be my husband,
to have and to hold from this day forward,
for better, for worse,
for richer, for poorer,
in sickness and in health,
to love and to cherish,
till death us do part,
according to God's holy law,
and this is my solemn vow

The words of the vows express the love that the bride and bridegroom have for each other. Note the word cherish, which is not a common word nowadays. To cherish means to show your appreciation for someone of great value to you. A husband and wife cherish each other by taking great care to seek the very best for each other.

These qualities of love are described in the following Bible passage, which is often read out at weddings:

> Love is patient and kind; love does not envy or boast; it is not arrogant or rude. It does not insist on its own way; it is not irritable or resentful; it does not rejoice at wrongdoing, but rejoices with the truth. Love bears all things, believes all things, hopes all things, endures all things. Love never ends.
>
> 1 Corinthians 13:4-8

This is the kind of love that the husband and wife are promising to share with each other when they make their vows.

More about love in marriage

The Bible gives us two special descriptions of how a husband should love his wife. He should do so in the same way that Christ loves His church and gave His life for the church (Ephesians 5:25). He should also love his wife as his own body

(Ephesians 5:28). In other words, the husband should look after his wife just as he looks after himself. What a challenge! Boys need to think about this carefully. It is not easy for them to be a husband as God intends.

The demands of marriage are equally challenging for the wife. She needs to be prepared to respect and submit to her husband (Ephesians 5:22) – so girls need to think carefully whether they are prepared to do this for the man they plan to marry.

Note that there are no 'ifs' or 'buts' in the vows of marriage. You promise to be devoted to your husband or wife, whatever circumstances develop. This is sometimes called unconditional love. You may marry a millionaire or an athlete, but you have promised to be faithful to them, even if all their money runs out or they end up in a wheelchair.

This kind of love is a decision to love the other person, so is not ultimately dependent on your feelings or what happens in the marriage. You simply promise to put the other person's interests before your own. This is very different from the kind of love that we often hear about on the television or read about in magazines, where people are often seen marrying and breaking up a few years later.

Finally, the words 'till death us do part' in the marriage vows are very important. God intends marriage to be life-long, only ending with the death of the husband or wife.

What are God's purposes for marriage?

The first should be obvious from what has been said about love in marriage. The husband and wife must love, care for and support each other. So your husband or wife should be your very best friend for life.

The second purpose for marriage is to have children. It is God's intention that children should benefit from being born and brought up in a family based on the security of marriage. A plant grows best when it has adequate amounts of water, food and sun. We know from studies that children do best in a married family.[1] Why might this be? Can you think of some of the reasons why a secure and happy marriage helps a child?

Remember the marriage vows. Think of the strength and help that children receive from knowing that they have a mother and father who have promised to keep on loving each other, whatever the circumstances.

---

1   See, for example, 'Why marriage matters: Thirty conclusions from social sciences' published in 2012 by Institute of American Values, available on-line from www.americanvalues.org